I'M REWIRING MY BRAIN:

MY JOURNEY TO FREEDOM

WORKBOOK

I'M REWIRING MY BRAIN:

MY JOURNEY TO FREEDOM

WORKBOOK

SBPC

SIMMS BOOKS PUBLISHING CORPORATION

SBPC

SIMMS BOOKS PUBLISHING CORP.
Publishers Since 2012

Published By Simms Books Publishing
Jonesboro, GA

Copyright © Dr. Kay Vonne Cason-Turner, 2022

All rights reserved. No part of this book may be reproduced, scanned, or distributed in any print or electronic form without permission. Please do not participate in or encourage piracy of copyrighted materials in violation of the author's rights. Purchase only authorized editions.

Library of Congress Cataloging in Publication Data

Dr. Kay Vonne Cason-Turner

I'm Rewiring My Brain: My Journey to Freedom Workbook

ISBN: 978-1-949433-33-3

Printed in the United States of America
Edited by Mary Hoekstra
Cover by: Nidia Roman, RomanArts

TABLE OF CONTENTS

INTRODUCTION..i

CHAPTER 1
YOUR JOURNEY BEGINS..1

CHAPTER 2
UNCONSCIOUS CHOICES AND HABITS............................5

CHAPTER 3
HOW WE DEVELOP HABITS..7

CHAPTER 4
YOU CAN CHANGE: REWIRE YOUR BRAIN.....................9

CHAPTER 5
PROGRAMS AS BELIEF SYSTEMS....................................11

CHAPTER 6
TRIGGERS..13
- SITUATIONAL TRIGGERS
- THOUGHTS AS TRIGGERS

CHAPTER 7
THOUGHT/FEELING CONNECTION..................................17

CHAPTER 8
RETICULAR ACTIVATING SYSTEM (RAS).......................19

CHAPTER 9
STRATEGIZE TO REWIRE YOUR BRAIN..........................21

CHAPTER 10

AFFIRMATIONS..23

CHAPTER 11
VISION BOARDS..25

CHAPTER 12
MEDITATION..27

CHAPTER 13
VISUALIZATIONS...31

CHAPTER 14
MINDFULNESS...35

CHAPTER 15
REINTERPRETING YOUR PAST...39

CHAPTER 16
IDENTIFY AND CHANGE YOUR PROGRAMS..41

CHAPTER 17
No Exercises. You get a break :)...TAKE A BREAK

CHAPTER 18
POSITIVE SUPPORT SYSTEM..43

CHAPTER 19
CONSCIOUS EFFORT: INVESTING YOUR TIME AND ENERGY INTO
YOURSELF..45

SUGGESTED OUTLINE FOR REWIRE YOUR BRAIN SUPPORT GROUP

Introduction

This workbook is a great step-by-step guide that will facilitate your success in rewiring your brain. It is most beneficial when you use it with its' complimentary book, "I Rewired My Brain: My Journey to Freedom," (Hopefully, you have read it). Completing the exercises in this workbook will help you to gain a greater understanding of yourself and as you follow through with the recommended practices it will help transform your life.

As your transformation unfolds, you consistently grow into being the best you that you can be. As a bonus, along the way, you will also resolve issues that contribute to your mental and emotional distress. To aid you in your success, this workbook has been designed to help you to be organized in your approach to your change and transformation. The chapters in this workbook correlate to the chapters in the 2nd part of the complimentary book. Before completing the chapter exercises in this workbook, you should read the corresponding chapter in the book, first. This will significantly enhance your growth potential because you will have a more in-depth understanding of the questions before you answer them.

The corresponding book gives you the information that you need to truly grasp the real importance as to why you should whole-heartedly put your time and energy into completing the exercises in this workbook. Understanding the significance of why you should rewire your brain, will greatly contribute to your success in completing these exercises, without it, you may not give a thoroughly thought-out answer. Not taking time to really give it some thought, you could be robbing yourself of meeting the person that you were born to be. If you have read the book, then you are well on your way to the next step in your journey. Writing things down often gives them more meaning. Being organized in your approach, as you write things down, helps those things to make more sense to you. As things make more sense to you, uncertainty and confusion wane, and you can move through life with greater knowledge, wisdom, and clarity.

Schedule some time in your day or week to work on the exercises in this workbook. There is no need for you to rush through it. Don't try to complete all of the chapters in one day. Take your time and contemplate, as this will be an unfolding learning process. The completion of this workbook is what lays the strong foundation for rewiring your brain. The process of rewiring your brain requires you to utilize the tools and regularly practice the strategies in this workbook. Remember, nerves that fire together, wire together.

*Embrace your journey of growth, healing, and change, as it can lead you to experience the inner peace, harmony, happiness, and Love that you desire and deserve! It's your time now! Level up! Rewire Your Brain!

CHAPTER 1

Your Journey Begins

Chapter 1
Your Journey Begins

Did you read the complimentary book "I Rewired My Brain: My Journey To Freedom?" Remember it is highly recommended that you read it before completing this workbook. If you did read the book, in the space provided below, write about the driving factors that led to reading it.

_____
_____
_____
_____
_____
_____
_____
_____

What aspects in your life are not going the way that you want? Identify things in your life that cause you to feel stress, anxiety, unhappiness, depression, anger and/or feel overwhelmed. Write about those things, in the space provided below.

_____
_____
_____
_____
_____
_____
_____

Imagine feeling peace and being happy. Imagine what your life looks like in this peaceful and happy state. Imagine the New You who is peaceful and happy. What is different about your life? Describe your new life in the space provided below.

_____
_____
_____
_____
_____
_____
_____
_____
_____

What is different about you, as a person?

_____
_____
_____
_____
_____
_____
_____
_____
_____

How much do you want to change? Circle the number on this scale of 1-10 that represents how much you want to change. 1 means just a little and 10 means a lot. 5 is in the middle. etc.

1   2   3   4   5   6   7   8   9   10

How committed are you to making changes in your life and in yourself?

1   2   3   4   5   6   7   8   9   10

In order to take this journey, you have to be totally honest with yourself. If your score is below 5, that's ok. You might not be ready for change yet, but it's good that you are completing this workbook and you're ready to take in information, so that when that time for change comes, you will be prepared.

Write your commitment number here _____

If your number is not 10 write what you might need to do to get yourself to the next highest number. For example, if you are at 5 what might you need to do to get to 6?

_____

_____

_____

_____

_____

_____

_____

_____

CHAPTER 2
Unconscious Choices and Habits

Chapter 2
Unconscious Choices and Habits

Write down some of your habits that you are aware of. Write down your good habits and your bad habits

Behavioral Habits

        Good Habits   Bad Habits

_____   _____
_____   _____
_____   _____
_____   _____
_____   _____
_____   _____
_____   _____
_____   _____

Habitual ways of thinking

        Good Habits   Bad Habits

_____   _____
_____   _____
_____   _____
_____   _____
_____   _____
_____   _____
_____   _____
_____   _____

CHAPTER 3

How We Develop Habits

Chapter 3

How We Develop Habits

Write down where some of your habits came from. For example, some of your habits will have come from things that you were taught as a child, by parents, caregivers, or teachers. Some habits resulted from you being around others and you started acting the way that they acted or thinking about things from their perspective. You might like some of your habits. You might dislike some of your habits. Nevertheless, write down the habit, then write down where you think it came from.

Habit	Where the habit originated

You can write down some of the habits from Chapter 2 in this workbook or you can write different habits.

CHAPTER 4

You Can Change:

Rewire Your Brain

Chapter 4
You Can Change: Rewire Your Brain

Identify what habits you want to change, then, beside each one, write down the new habit that you want to replace it with.

Habit you want to change	New Replacement Habit
_____	_____
_____	_____
_____	_____
_____	_____
_____	_____
_____	_____
_____	_____
_____	_____
_____	_____
_____	_____

*****Practice the Replacement Habit Regularly

CHAPTER 5
Programs as Belief Systems

Chapter 5
Programs as Belief Systems

Identify your belief systems that are not taking you where you want to go in life. Then identify what new belief systems you want to replace them with.

Current Unproductive Belief System 　　New Replacement Program/Belief System

_____　　_____
_____　　_____
_____　　_____
_____　　_____
_____　　_____
_____　　_____
_____　　_____
_____　　_____
_____　　_____

When you realize that your current unproductive belief system is in your thoughts, make yourself focus on your new replacement belief system. When you do this regularly, your new replacement belief system will become your belief system and the unproductive belief system that you had will go away.

*****Practice this replacement process regularly. Take a picture of this page with your cell phone so that you can have it with you. Review it daily so that you can remember the belief systems and the replacements.

CHAPTER 6

Triggers:

•Situational Triggers

Chapter 6   Triggers:
1. Situational Triggers

Identify situations that trigger you. Then, identify the negative habits that those situations activate.

Situation   Activated Habit

1. _____   _____
2. _____   _____
3. _____   _____
4. _____   _____
5. _____   _____

For the items listed above, identify the Replacement Habit, whether it is behavioral or a mindset/perspective and write it down below.

Replacement Habit

1. _____
2. _____
3. _____
4. _____
5. _____

*****Practice employing the Replacement Habits regularly

Thoughts as Triggers

Identify some of the stinkin' thinkin' that you tend to engage in that gets you triggered/worked up. If you have a current issue going on now, write that down. If you don't have a current issue, then write down your stinkin' thinkin' from a past issue that sometimes bothers you. Then, answer the questions: Is it true (circle yes or no), How do I know it is 100% true (of course if you circled "no" there is no need to answer this question). Then identify a mantra to focus on instead of focusing on the stinkin' thinkin'. Remember that just because you think about something does not mean that the thought is true. You are just focusing on thoughts.

Stinkin' Thinkin' Issue	Is it true?	How do I know it is 100% true?
1._____	Yes No	_____
2._____	Yes No	_____
3._____	Yes No	_____
4._____	Yes No	_____

Mantra (Create a mantra for your stinkin' thinkin' that you have listed above)

1._____
2._____
3._____
4._____

******When the thought triggers pop into your head, don't focus on the thoughts (stinkin' thinkin'), instead say your mantra. Do this every time the thought triggers surface.

You can employ distractions when you have a difficult time getting the stinkin' thinkin' out of your head using the mantra. Sometimes one strategy does not work and you have to employ a plan B and sometimes a plan C to get your thoughts under your control.

Identify some enjoyable or interesting distractions that you can focus on, rather than focusing on stinkin' thinkin'. List some distractions below.

1. _____
2. _____
3. _____
4. _____
5. _____
6. _____
7. _____
8. _____
9. _____
10. _____
11. _____
12. _____
13. _____
14. _____
15. _____

CHAPTER 7

Thought/Feeling Connection

Chapter 7
Thought/Feeling Connection

When you focus on thoughts, emotions/feelings arise. If you focus on negative or destructive thoughts, distressing emotions arise. If you focus on positive or productive thoughts, desirable or comfortable feelings arise.

Think of something that you don't like that is occurring, or that has already happened. Write down that situation.

_____
_____
_____

Now, focus on that situation. Think about all of the things that you don't like about that situation. Think about what bothers you most about that situation. Now write down the different emotions that you are experiencing, such as sadness, anger, anxiety, frustration, hopelessness, or feeling overwhelmed and powerless.

_____   _____   _____
_____   _____   _____

Now, think of something that is occurring, or has already happened, that you do like, something that you truly desire, something that you are very pleased about.

Write down that situation below

_____
_____
_____
_____

Now, focus on that situation. Think about all of the things that you like about that situation. Think about those aspects of the situation that you are pleased with.

Now, write down the emotions/feelings that you are experiencing. Examples; happiness, excitement, contentment, joy, peace, calm, serenity, and so on.

_____   _____   _____

_____   _____   _____

Now, make up a scenario about something bad happening in your life. This scenario has not happened, it is totally made up. Nevertheless, this bad scenario is not anything that you want to experience. Think about it for a while. Now, in the space below, write down the emotions that you are experiencing.

_____   _____   _____

_____   _____   _____

*****Now you are consciously aware of how your thoughts affect how you feel. It does not matter if the thoughts are based upon something that has happened or if it is a totally made up story. Regardless, whatever thoughts you focus on, you will experience emotions that are consistent with the thoughts.

*******Now, make up an exciting situation and focus on that. This situation is truly something that makes your heart sing. This situation makes you feel really good. Be with that good feeling and smile, smile, smile.

CHAPTER 8
Reticular Activating System (RAS)

Chapter 8
Reticular Activating System (RAS)

It's time to give your Reticular Activating System a command. Go to Chapter 4 in this workbook. List your new replacement habits. If you think of more new replacement habits, write those down, as well. **Begin each line with "I will" then write your replacement habit.**

My New Replacement Habits

1. _____
2. _____
3. _____
4. _____
5. _____
6. _____
7. _____
8. _____

-Take a pic of your list with your cell phone so that you will always have it with you.

-Read your list at least 2 times a day

-Start paying more attention to how you move through life

-As time passes, make mental notes as you become aware of your RAS in action.

CHAPTER 9
Strategize to Rewire Your Brain

Chapter 9
Strategize to Rewire Your Brain

It's Show Time!

Are you ready to be in the driver's seat of your life, even more than you have been in the past? Or, do you want to joy ride and let your current programs drive you through life?

If you are ready to consciously create the life experiences that you desire, then make a commitment to yourself.

Complete, sign and date the contract on the next page, from you, for you, by you!

*****After you sign your contract, read it aloud to your Self with conviction. Read it daily. Rewire your brain!

My Contract to My Self to Rewire My Brain

I _____ make a commitment to my Self to live my life more consciously. I commit to practicing strategies to rewire my brain on a daily basis. My signing of this contract is my dedication to my Self to grow and to develop my Self to be the best Me that I can be. I am ready to live my best life! This is my vow to my Self! I commit to change! I will rewire my brain!

_____   _____
Signature   Date

CHAPTER 10

Affirmations

Chapter 10
Affirmations

Identify 10 Affirmations.

1. _____
2. _____
3. _____
4. _____
5. _____
6. _____
7. _____
8. _____
9. _____
10. _____

-Read your affirmations daily, at least 2 times a day.

-Take a pic of them with your cell phone.

-Go the extra mile and record yourself saying your affirmations with a background of music, soundscapes or tones.

-Listen to your recordings daily

********If you can't think of your own affirmations, search for affirmations on the internet. Find affirmations that speak to Your soul!

CHAPTER 11

Vision Boards

Chapter 11
Vision Boards

What areas of your life do you want to change?

Write a list of ideas for your vision boards.

For example; Relationship, Health, Finances, Education, Career

1._____
2._____
3._____
4._____
5._____
7._____
8._____
9._____
10._____

After you have generated your list, identify what vision board you want to complete first and do it.

***Remember my daughter's strategy; don't glue, take pics. If you take pics, you can use some of the same images, words and letters over and over again!

CHAPTER 12

Meditation

Chapter 12
Meditation

Schedule a time and place where you will meditate.

Time _____

Place _____

When will you start?

Date _____

Will you use music?   Yes   No   Not Sure

If so, what kind of music? _____

How long will you meditate, 5 minutes, 10 minutes or more? Write how long you plan to meditate.

I plan to meditate for _____ minutes.

Use the next few pages to journal about your meditation experiences. If you decide to continue journaling, you can order the *I'm Rewiring My Brain; My Journey to Freedom* journal to record your journey, or you can use something different. Documenting your journey is a good way to realize your growth and transformation!

My Meditation Experience

Date _____

Time _____

Experience

_____
_____
_____
_____
_____
_____

Date _____

Time _____

Experience

_____
_____
_____
_____
_____
_____

My Meditation Experience

Date _____
Time _____

Experience

_____
_____
_____
_____
_____
_____
_____

Date _____
Time _____

Experience

_____
_____
_____
_____
_____
_____
_____

My Meditation Experience

Date _____

Time _____

Experience

_____
_____
_____
_____
_____
_____

Date _____

Time _____

Experience

_____
_____
_____
_____
_____
_____

CHAPTER 13

Visualizations

Chapter 13
Visualizations

What transformations in your life do you want to visualize? Visualize them as if they are occurring right now. Allow the inner movie to play on the big screen of your mind. Feel it! Enjoy it! Allow joy and gratitude to permeate your being.

Transformations that I will Visualize

1._____
2._____
3._____
4._____
5._____
6._____
7._____
8._____

Use the next few pages to journal about your visualizations and your experiences. If you decide to continue journaling, and you have not yet ordered your *I'm Rewiring My Brain; My Journey to Freedom* journal, then you can order it today, or either use something different to write in. Whatever you choose, document your journey. The journaling process actually adds more to your realizations and transformation.

My Visualization Experience

Date_____

Time_____

My Experience

_____
_____
_____
_____
_____
_____

Date_____

Time_____

My Experience

_____
_____
_____
_____
_____
_____

My Visualization Experience

Date_____

Time_____

My Experience

_____
_____
_____
_____
_____

Date_____

Time_____

My Experience

_____
_____
_____
_____
_____
_____

My Visualization Experience

Date_____

Time_____

My Experience

_____
_____
_____
_____
_____
_____

Date_____

Time_____

My Experience

_____
_____
_____
_____
_____
_____

CHAPTER 14

Mindfulness

Chapter 14
Mindfulness

Identify what mindfulness exercises* you will practice.

1. _____
2. _____
3. _____
4. _____
5. _____

*Remember that some exercises are included in the book and you can find other exercises on the internet.

*Practice the exercises daily

Day by day, pay attention to how your awareness is increasing.
On the next page, document your experiences with the mindfulness exercises and your growing awareness of being more attuned to the goings on around you and within you.

***PS: By now you are probably thinking that all of this writing and journaling takes too much time; it does not fit into your busy schedule. Think about this: Investing your time and energy and often your money into yourself is paramount to change. You give your time to others and now it's time to give it to yourself.

My Mindfulness Experiences

Date_____

Time_____

My Mindfulness Experience

_____
_____
_____
_____
_____
_____

Date_____

Time_____

My Mindfulness Experience

_____
_____
_____
_____
_____
_____

My Mindfulness Experiences

Date_____

Time_____

My Mindfulness Experience

_____
_____
_____
_____
_____
_____

Date_____

Time_____

My Mindfulness Experience

_____
_____
_____
_____
_____
_____

My Mindfulness Experiences

Date_____

Time_____

My Mindfulness Experience

_____
_____
_____
_____
_____
_____

Date_____

Time_____

My Mindfulness Experience

_____
_____
_____
_____
_____
_____

CHAPTER 15

Reinterpreting Your Past

Chapter 15
Reinterpreting Your Past

Think of something from your past that leads to you feeling bad when you think about it. Now, with the conscious intention of giving that situation a different, productive meaning, reinterpret that situation.

Every obstacle is an opportunity for growth. Turn your lemons into lemonade. Rise up to a higher perspective. You might have to step out of that situation and look at it as an observer. Even if you come up with something like, "Everything happens for a reason," or one of my favorites, "Everything is in divine order," those perspectives will likely not leave you feeling bad or distressed.

Write about the situation and how it currently leads to you feeling bad (hurt, angry, sad etc.) and then write your reinterpretation of the situation.

The situation that I feel bad about:

_____
_____
_____
_____
_____
_____
_____
_____
_____

My Productive Reinterpretation of the Situation

_____
_____
_____
_____
_____
_____
_____
_____
_____

***You should feel better when you focus on the reinterpreted version of the story. Reinterpreting a situation takes insight (being better able to really see from a higher mindset, the cause-and-effect dynamics in a situation). Reinterpreting situations leads to growth and more inner peace.

Sometimes reinterpreting is like peeling the layers of an onion. You get to one layer of your interpretation only to find out that there are more, deeper layers of the situation that reveals more information. The reinterpretation process unfolds and expands allowing you to see things differently.

I am reminded of what my spiritual teacher taught me about forgiveness. She said that forgiveness is not something that you do, it is what happens when you understand, hence it is a process of unfolding and unveiling until you have that *Ah ha* moment!

CHAPTER 16
Identify and Change Your Programs

Chapter 16
Identify and Change Your Programs

Chapters 4 and 5 of this workbook contain the exercises for identifying and changing your programs. After completing the exercises, it is very important to practice implementing your new, desired habits/programs on a regular basis.

Practice. Practice. Practice. Victory is yours!

CHAPTER 17

No Exercises.

You get a break

CHAPTER 18

Positive Support System

Chapter 18
Positive Support System

Identify your ideas for a support system and write about how you think having the support system might benefit you.

_____
_____
_____
_____

Identify who or what might be the opposite of a support system and remember not to try to get them to be your support system.

_____
_____
_____
_____

CHAPTER 19

Conscious Effort: Investing Your Time and Energy into Yourself

Chapter 19

Conscious Effort: Investing Your Time and Energy Into Yourself

You are worthy of your time and energy. It is extremely important to invest in yourself. Write about how you will continue to invest your time and your energy into rewiring your brain and how you expect this process to change your life.

_____
_____
_____
_____
_____
_____
_____
_____

Now, read aloud what you wrote, and at the end, proclaim with conviction,
"I GOT THIS! I CAN, I WILL, SUCCEED!"

CONGRATULATIONS!

SUGGESTED OUTLINE FOR REWIRE YOUR BRAIN SUPPORT GROUP

Suggested Outline for Rewire Your Brain Support Group

Time:

- Recommended time for a group is 1 ½ to 2 hours depending on the size of the group.

Group size:

- 1 ½ hour group should consist of no more than 5 people
- 2-hour group should consist of no more than 6-8 people.

Structure:

- You need a facilitator; A person who controls the flow of the group. One who makes sure that everyone has a chance to speak, only if they want to speak. Only one person speaks at a time, as they will be sharing the most intimate details of their experience.

Duties:

- The Facilitator should set a time limit for each person speaking, to stay within the time limit of the group, so as to be considerate of each other's schedule. Make arrangements in the event that more time is needed to address those who need it and schedule another day to continue.

- If the group meetings are face to face, it needs to be in a space wherein there will be no interruptions, as people will need to feel emotionally safe, relaxed, and comfortable. *The same thing follows even if meetings are on video apps, such as Zoom, Google Meet, and or GoToMeeting.

Things to remember:
- Each person should come comfortably dressed.
- Everyone should bring their Rewire My Brain Book, Workbook, and a Journal.
- Bring an ink pen or something to write with.
- **All cell phones and devices should be silenced
- **It is better if people are fully present, not eating or snacking during the group session.

If the meeting is in person:
- Make sure there is tissue for tearfulness.
- Everyone should sit in a circle so that everyone is facing each other. Group members must be able to see each other as each one shares.
- Facilitator welcomes everyone
- Everyone says their name.
- The facilitator again welcomes everyone and shares that the group is coming together to embark upon a journey of change.

**The creed is read to set the intentions and tone for the meeting.
**The creed should be emailed to all members before the first meeting.

The facilitator starts the creed:

"During this time and in this space, we come together as one

To share our thoughts, feelings, emotions, and beliefs

To discover where we are,

and to ultimately choose who, what, and where we want to be.

We collectively hold the vision for the manifestation of each other's dreams!"

Everyone together

I commit to this life-changing journey

Of rewiring my brain

I will break my chains

And give birth to the greatest version of My Self.

I now proclaim my freedom!

First meeting:
- Group members share their overall experience of the book and why they read the book.

    *It is better if all participants have read the entire book.

Subsequent meetings:
- The following meetings should cover two chapters from the workbook. If time does not allow covering two chapters, for some of the meetings, cover 1 chapter.
- The workbook exercises should be completed before the meetings.
- Group members can talk about their experience of answering the questions. They can share what they wrote, and talk about why they wrote it if they want to share. Members can share their "Aha" experiences.
- Members can journal, taking notes during the meeting if something stands out for them.
- Members can share their "takeaways" from the meeting.

The Close-out:

After everyone who has wanted to share, has shared, and the allotted time has come, it is time for the close-out.

- Have someone share a quote, short poem, or a prayer of their choice at the end of the group meeting.
- The facilitator closes by thanking everyone for coming to the Rewire Your Brain Support group meeting. The facilitator shares the date, time, and place for the next meeting.
- To end the meeting, the facilitator says, **"We are breaking our chains!"**

Everyone Together

"We are on our Journey to Freedom!"

www.ingramcontent.com/pod-product-compliance
Lightning Source LLC
Chambersburg PA
CBHW081501070526
44586CB00019B/2449